Presented to:

_____

by:

_____

on:

_____

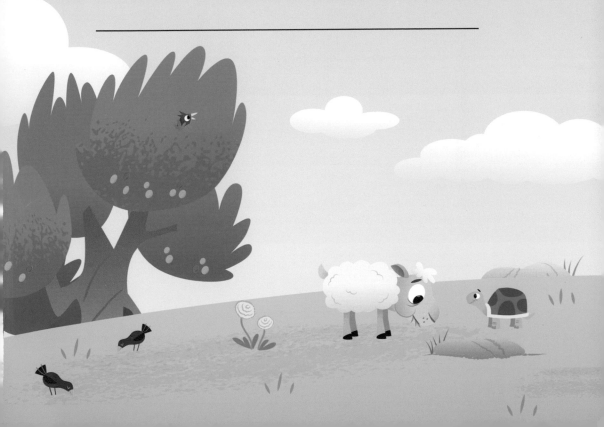

YouVersion   OneHope
GOD'S WORD. EVERY CHILD.

The Bible App for Kids™ Storybook Bible
Created by YouVersion® and OneHope, Inc.

Copyright © 2015 OneHope, Inc.
Text, Illustration and Graphic Design Copyright © 2015 by OneHope, Inc.

The Bible App for Kids™ and YouVersion® are trademarks of LifeChurch.tv.

ISBN English 978-1-63049-065-2
ISBN Church Edition 978-1-63049-127-7

All Bible stories are paraphrased from the HOLY BIBLE: EASY-TO-READ VERSION © 2001
by Bible League International.

Permission requests should be addressed to:
OneHope, Inc.
600 SW 3rd St
Pompano Beach, FL 33060
www.onehope.net

Publishing in partnership with Winters Publishing Group, 2448 E 81st Suite 5900,
Tulsa, OK 74137

Printed in China
10 9 8 7 6 5 4 3 2 1

The Bible App
FOR KIDS
STORYBOOK BIBLE

Created by YouVersion and OneHope, the Bible App for Kids is sharing God's Story with children all around the world. You can interact with all the stories in this book – as well as many others – in the app. Each story comes alive with animation, narration, and music. Download the free Bible App for Kids on the App Store, Google Play, and Amazon Appstore, or visit bible.com/kids from your mobile device or tablet.

Table of Contents

In the beginning, God made everything out of nothing! He made us to know Him and to love Him.

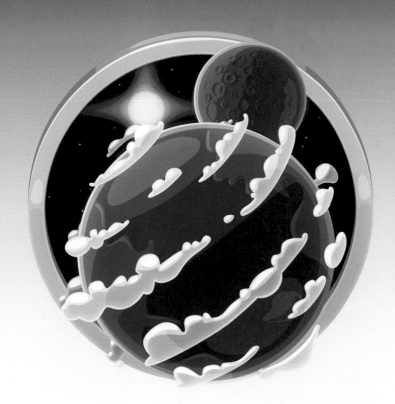

In the Beginning

Creation of the World
Genesis 1:1–2:4

We live in a beautiful world! Just look at the amazing things around you.

Let's go back to the beginning and see what the Bible tells us about how it all began.

In the beginning, God made the heavens and the earth. God moved over the darkness and said, "Light!"

He called the light "Day" and
He called the darkness "Night."

Day One!
Done!

Then God made a space to separate
the waters above from the waters below.
He called the space "Sky."

Day Two! Done!

God gathered the waters together, and dry ground appeared. He called the ground "Land" and the waters "Seas." Then he made plants like grass, grain, and trees.

Day Three! Done!

Then God made lights in the sky.
He made the sun for the day, the
moon for the night, and all the stars.

Day Four!
Done!

God made fish to swim in the waters and birds to fly in the sky. "Have babies!" He told them. "Fill the world with splashing and singing."

Day Five!
Done!

17

Next, God made animals. He made
farm animals, wild animals, and
animals that crawl
on the ground.

"Just one more thing to make," God said,

"the most special thing of all."

So, in His image, God made man and woman. "Have babies," He said. "Take charge of the world. Care for the fish, the birds, and the animals."

Day Six!
Done!

Then God looked at everything He had made. "It's very good!" He said. So on the seventh day, He rested and made that day special.

Day Seven! Done!

What was God's most special creation?

God was very pleased with everything He made. There was no pain or death. Everything was good. Then God gave the first man and woman a rule to obey.

The First Sin

The Fall
Genesis 3:1-24

The first man and woman, Adam and Eve, lived in a beautiful garden that God made for them.

But Satan came as a crafty serpent
and tempted Adam and Eve...

27

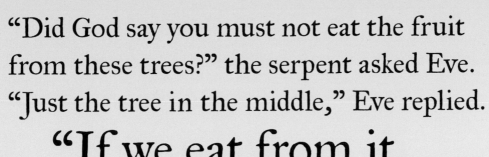

"Did God say you must not eat the fruit from these trees?" the serpent asked Eve. "Just the tree in the middle," Eve replied. **"If we eat from it, we'll die."**

"You won't die!" said the serpent. "There's a reason why God doesn't want you to eat from that tree. If you do, you'll be like Him. You'll know what He knows!"

Eve ate the fruit. She gave some to Adam, who was with her. He ate it too. And at once, they knew things they had never known before.

One thing they knew was
that they were naked!

They sewed leaves together to cover themselves. They'd never felt fear or shame before, so they knew something was wrong.

"Adam!" God called. "Eve!"
"We're hiding," said Adam.
"We're naked."

"You know that because you ate from the tree," God sighed. Then Adam blamed Eve, and Eve blamed the serpent.

God said, "Serpent, you must crawl on your belly. A woman's son will defeat you.

Eve, childbirth will be painful.
Adam, growing food will be difficult."

Then God made clothes for Adam and Eve and sent them out of the garden. He put an angel with a flaming sword there, so they could not return.

What happened when Adam and Eve ate the fruit from the tree in the middle of the garden?

Sin broke our relationship with God, our loving Creator. But God still loved us. From the start, He had a wonderful plan.

Two by Two

Noah and the Flood
Genesis 6:5-9:17

The earth filled up with people, but they sinned so much that God was sorry He had made them.

He decided to send a flood to wash away everyone on earth.

There was a man named Noah
who wasn't like the others.

Noah loved God and obeyed Him.

God decided to spare Noah and his family from the flood.

God warned Noah about the flood.
He told him to build an enormous boat
with a low roof, three decks, a window,
and a door.

In obedience, Noah built it.

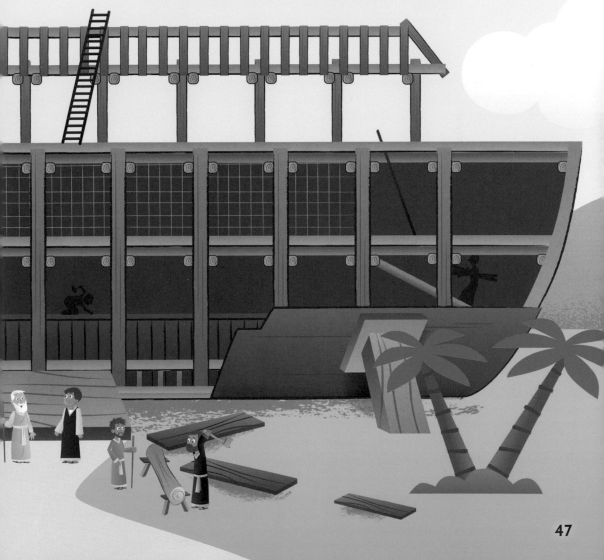

God told Noah to collect two of every kind of animal. One male. One female.

Then Noah, his family, and the animals went into the boat. God shut the door.

It rained for forty days and forty nights. Water fell from the sky and rose from the oceans and lakes. Even the tallest mountains disappeared beneath the flood.

Meanwhile, Noah, his family, and all the animals were safe in the boat, floating on the flood waters. God had not forgotten about Noah, not even for a moment.

God sent a wind to blow. The waters went down. The boat rested on Mount Ararat.

Noah sent out a dove. When it didn't return, he knew it was safe.

When the ground was dry, God told them to come out. He put a rainbow in the sky as a promise that

He would never flood the whole earth again.

What did the rainbow in the sky mean?

God's wonderful plan was to fix everything broken by sin. His plan continued with Abraham, a man who trusted God, and who became the father of the nation of Israel.

God's Amazing Promise

Abraham is Called by God
Genesis 12:1-9; 15:1-7

Abraham lived in Haran. "Abraham," God said, "I want you to leave Haran and go to another land."

God didn't tell Abraham where that was.
"Trust Me,"
God said.

"Do this," God said, "and your children will become a great nation!"

"How?" Abraham wondered. His wife, Sarah, was too old to have children.

"Trust Me," God said.

"Go where I tell you," God said, "and you will have more descendants than there are stars in the sky! They will bless the whole world. Trust Me."

So Abraham trusted God.

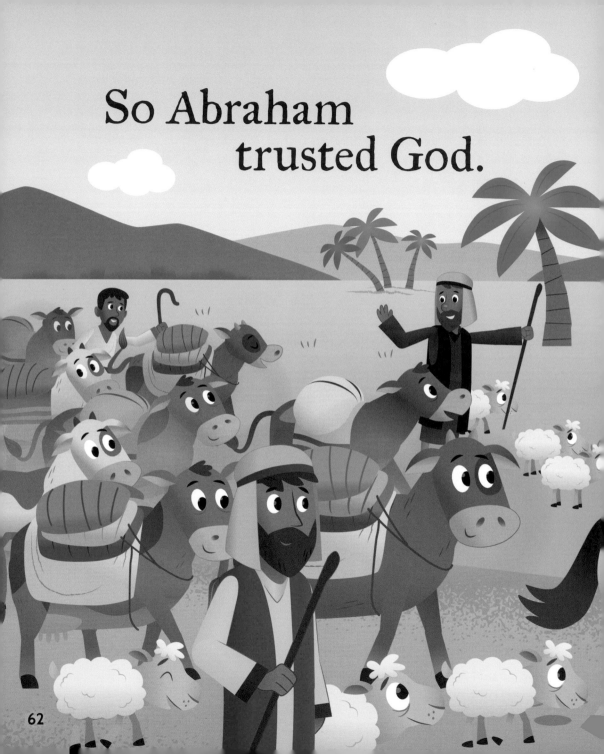

He took Sarah, his nephew, Lot, and everything they owned. He went where God told him to go. He went to the land of Canaan.

When he arrived, Abraham camped at Shechem. God appeared to him!

"I will give this land to you and your children," God said. Abraham built an altar to God there.

Abraham traveled around God's promised land. He was glad that he had trusted God. So he built another altar and gave thanks to God for all he had been promised.

How did Abraham respond to God's amazing promise?

*Abraham trusted God to keep
His promises, even when those
promises seemed impossible,
and even when God told him
to do something really hard.*

Abraham's Big Test

Abraham and Isaac
Genesis 15:1-6; 21:1-7; 22:1-19

God promised Abraham a son and, from that son, many descendants, who would bless the whole world.

But Abraham and his wife, Sarah, were
too old to have children.

Twenty years went by. Still, Abraham trusted God's promise. When he was 100 and Sarah was 90, God reminded them of His promise.

Sarah was going
to have a baby!

73

When their son was born, Sarah was so joyful that she laughed. "God has brought me laughter!" she said.

So they named their son Isaac, which means "he laughs."

When Isaac was a boy, God tested Abraham by telling him to take Isaac to Mount Moriah and kill him as a sacrifice to God. Abraham was confused, but still **he trusted God.**

Isaac carried the wood, and Abraham held the knife and the torch. Together they climbed the mountain. "Where is the lamb for the sacrifice?" asked Isaac.

"God will provide it," Abraham replied.

Abraham arranged the wood on an altar, tied up Isaac, and laid him on the wood. As he raised the knife to kill Isaac, an angel called his name:

"Don't hurt the boy!" the angel cried.
"God knows you
trust His promise.

Look, there in the bushes! A ram is caught by its horns! Sacrifice that instead."

So Abraham sacrificed the ram
instead of his son. He called the
place "God Will Provide," because
God provided the sacrifice.
Just as God had said,

His promise
came true.

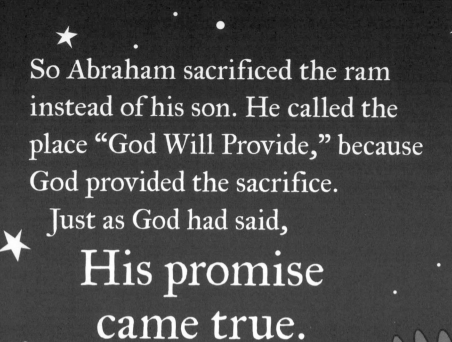

How did God provide for Abraham?

83

Isaac had a son named Jacob. God changed Jacob's name to Israel. Israel and his children went to the land of Egypt, where they grew into a great nation.

A Baby and a Bush

The Birth of Moses and the Burning Bush
Exodus 1:6–2:15; 3:1-15; 4:1-17

Egypt was filled with Israelites. The new Pharaoh was afraid that the Israelites would become too powerful.

So he made them
slaves and treated
them very badly.

Pharaoh ordered that all baby Israelite boys had to be killed. One woman put her baby in a basket and hid him by the river's edge. His sister watched him.

Pharaoh's daughter was bathing by the river. She found the baby and decided to keep him. His sister offered their mother's help to care for him.

Pharaoh's daughter named him Moses.

Moses grew up. One day he saw
an Egyptian beating an Israelite.

Moses killed the Egyptian. Then
he fled to Midian and was a shepherd
for forty years.

Moses was watching his sheep on Mount Horeb. The voice of God spoke from a burning bush.

"My people are suffering, Moses.
I have chosen you
to free them."

"I can't!" Moses cried.

"I'll help you,"

God promised. "Throw down your staff."
Moses did. It turned into a snake. When
he picked it up, it was a staff again.

"Put your hand in your cloak," God said.
Moses did. He looked. It was covered with
disease. When he did it again, it was healed.
"Show Pharaoh that!" God said.

"I'm not a good speaker," said Moses.
"I'll give you the words," God said.
"Your brother Aaron can help." So Moses
went to tell Pharaoh to set the
Israelites free.

What did God ask Moses to do?

God saw His people. He heard their cries. He was always with them. He remembered His promises to them. And because He loved them, this is how He saved them.

Let My People Go!

The Plagues and the Passover
Exodus 7:14-12:32

Moses and Aaron told Pharaoh, "The God of the Israelites says you must let His people go free.

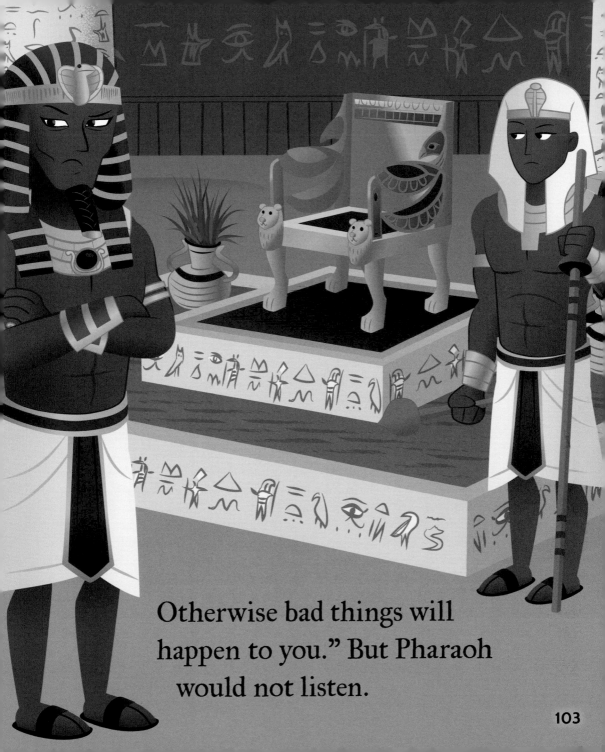

Otherwise bad things will
happen to you." But Pharaoh
would not listen.

So God turned the water in Egypt into blood. No one could drink it. Then He filled the Egyptian houses with frogs. Frogs were everywhere! Still Pharaoh would not listen.

So God filled the skies of Egypt with gnats. They covered the people like dust. Then He struck the land of Egypt with flies. Still Pharaoh would not listen.

So God killed the animals of Egypt. Horses, donkeys, camels, sheep, cows, and goats all died. Then He covered the Egyptian people with sores.

Still Pharaoh would not listen.

God sent hail to crush the crops of Egypt. Their barley and flax were destroyed.

Then He sent locusts to eat what fruit remained. Still **Pharaoh would not listen.**

So God sent darkness over the land.

But again, Pharaoh would not listen. God said, "I will kill every firstborn son in Egypt, and all the firstborn of the animals."

"My people must kill a lamb, eat it, and put its blood on their doorposts.

I will see the blood and pass over their houses.

Those children
will not die."

"You will call this
Passover and always
remember it." The Israelites obeyed God,
but the Egyptian firstborn sons died –
even Pharaoh's son.

Finally Pharaoh listened.
He let the Israelites go.

Why did God strike
Egypt with plagues?

God brought His people out
of slavery. He led them in a pillar
of cloud by day and in a pillar
of fire by night.

God Makes a Way

The Parting of the Red Sea and
The 10 Commandments
Exodus 14; 16:11-16; 17:1-7; 19-20

After Pharaoh's son died in the tenth plague, he let the Israelites leave.

They were near the Red Sea when
Pharaoh changed his mind again
and chased after them.

When the Israelites saw Pharaoh's chariots, they were terrified. But God told Moses to raise his staff toward the Red Sea.

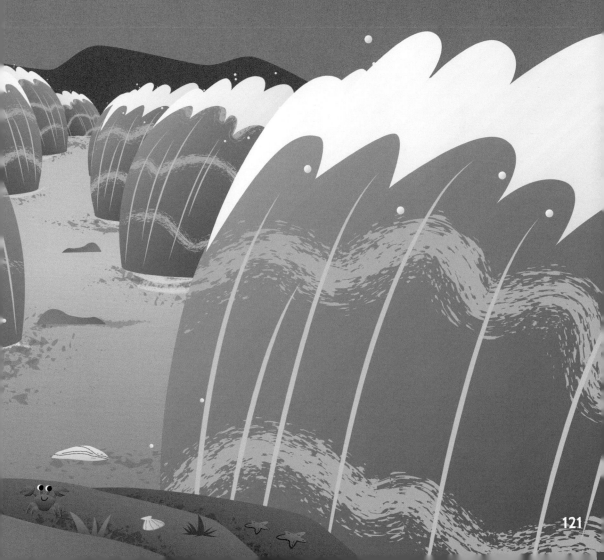

God sent a strong wind
and parted the sea!

A dry path appeared, and the Israelites
walked straight through the Red Sea!

There was a wall of water on each side of them. They arrived safely on the other side.

Pharaoh and his army followed them into the sea. God told Moses to stretch out his hand. Then the sea rolled back again.

Pharaoh and his army all drowned.

God led his people through a wilderness.
He fed them and
gave them water.

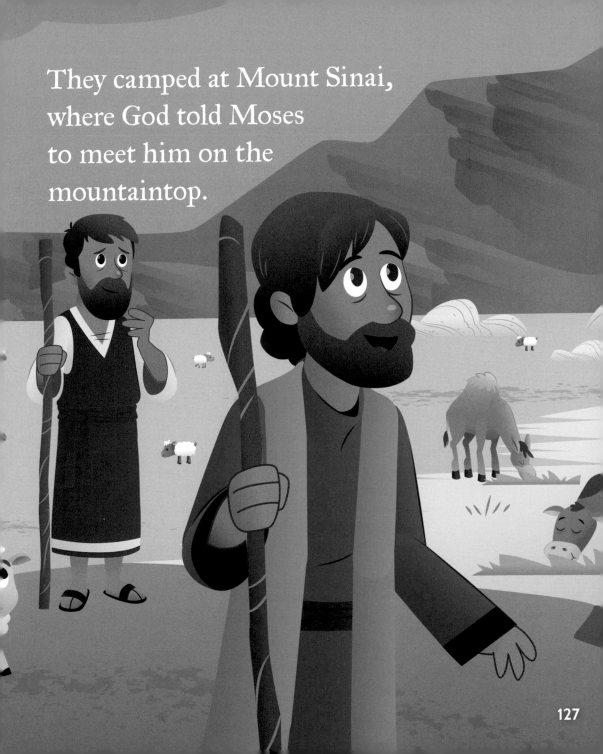

They camped at Mount Sinai, where God told Moses to meet him on the mountaintop.

Surrounded by fire and smoke, Moses climbed to the top, and God came down to meet him. Then God gave Moses the

Ten Commandments
on two stone tablets:

Don't worship other gods. Don't make idols.
Treat my name with respect.
Treat the Sabbath day as a special day.

129

Respect your parents. Don't murder.
Be loyal to your husband or your wife.
Don't steal. Don't lie. Don't envy people
or what they own.

Now the people knew how to obey God.

How did God show His love to His people?

God's people disobeyed His commandments, but He still loved them. After many years, He led them into the promised land. God provided for His people and brought others into His bigger story.

Wherever You Go

Ruth

Ruth 1-2; 4:9-17

A famine came to Israel. Elimelech, Naomi, and their sons went to Moab to find food. Elimelech died.

The sons married Moabite women, Orpah and Ruth. Then the sons died too.

The three women had no husbands.
When the famine in Israel was over,
Naomi decided to go home.

"Stay in Moab," she said to her daughters-in-law. "It's your home."

Orpah stayed. But Ruth said, "Wherever you go, I will go. Your people will be my people.

Your God will be my God."

Together Ruth and Naomi
went back to Israel.

It was harvest time in Israel. Naomi told Ruth to gather the bits of grain left behind in a field. The field belonged to Boaz, Elimelech's relative. Boaz approached Ruth.

"You were very kind to Naomi," Boaz said.
"Leaving home must have been hard. May
God bless you." He gave Ruth food and told
his workers to watch over her.

Ruth told Naomi what happened. Naomi smiled. "When someone dies, his closest relative cares for his family.

That person is their kinsman-redeemer.
Boaz is our kinsman-redeemer.
Stay close to him!"

So Ruth stayed close to Boaz. He liked her more each day. Boaz bought Elimelech's land

144

and took care of Naomi and Ruth.
Then he asked Ruth to marry him.

Ruth had a son called Obed. Obed's son was Jesse, Jesse's son was David, and David became Israel's greatest king!

So God blessed Ruth
just as Boaz had prayed.

How did God take care of Ruth?

David loved God from the time
he was a child. He sang a song
to God that went something like
this: "When the valley is dark,
I will not be afraid, for you
are by my side."

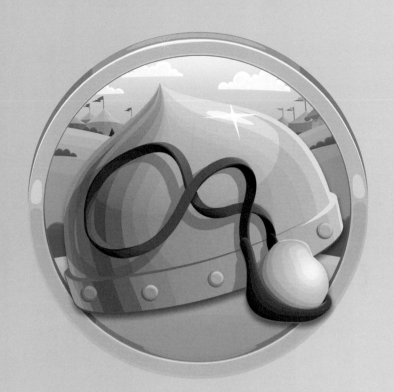

Stones, Slings, and Giant Things

David and Goliath
1 Samuel 16-17

Israel's first king was named Saul. King Saul did not obey God. So God said to Samuel, the prophet, "Find a man named Jesse. One of his sons will be the new king."

Samuel found Jesse in Bethlehem.
He looked at seven of Jesse's sons. They
looked handsome and strong. "Not them,"
God said. "I don't care about looks.

I care about what's in a person's heart."

Jesse sent for his youngest son, David, who was tending sheep in the fields. Samuel saw him and God said,

"He is the one!"

So David was anointed the new king.

Some time later, Israel fought the Philistines. A giant Philistine soldier called Goliath challenged the Israelites to send a champion to fight him.

But the Israelites were all too afraid.

David brought food to his brothers
in the army. He heard Goliath's
challenge and was not afraid.

"How dare he defy God's army?" asked David.
"I will fight him!"

Surprised, King Saul offered David his armor. "No," said David. "God helped me kill wild beasts. He will help me against Goliath too!"

David took five stones
and a sling.

"Am I a dog?" Goliath roared. "You send this stick of a boy to fight me!"

160

"You have a spear," said David,
"but I have the help of Israel's God!"

David put a stone into the sling and threw it.

It struck Goliath's forehead and knocked him down. The Israelites defeated the Philistines. With God's help, David was a hero!

Who helped David bring down Goliath?

165

David continued to serve King Saul for many years. When King Saul died, David became king, then there were many kings after David. As time passed, God's people turned away from the Lord. So God sent prophets to remind them to worship Him, the one true God.

Fire From Heaven

Elijah
1 Kings 16:29–17:1; 18:1; 17–39

D avid became a great king. Then his son Solomon reigned. After Solomon died, God's people had many bad kings.

King Ahab was one
of the worst. His wife, Jezebel,
worshipped the false god, Baal.

Jezebel persuaded Ahab and God's people to worship Baal too. Because of their sins,

God stopped the rain for several years. Then He sent His prophet Elijah to King Ahab.

"You have disobeyed God and worshipped Baal," Elijah said. "Tell everyone, including the prophets of Baal,

to meet me on Mount Carmel.
I will prove who the
true God is!"

Everyone gathered on the mountain. Then Elijah said to the people, "Make up your mind! If the Lord is God, follow Him. However, if Baal proves himself today, follow him."

"Baal's prophets and I will each kill a bull, place it on an altar, and pray. The god that sends fire to burn up the bull is

the true God!"

Baal's prophets went first. They prayed to Baal all morning. No fire came.

"Maybe Baal is sleeping," Elijah laughed. "Shout louder!" So Baal's prophets shouted all afternoon. Still, nothing happened.

Elijah built an altar.
He put the bull and
the wood on it.

He dug a ditch around it. Then he poured water over everything until the ditch was full!

Elijah prayed. Immediately fire fell from heaven! It burned up the bull, the wood, the stones, and the water! The people bowed down and cried, "The Lord is God!"

How did Elijah show the people that the Lord is God?

Sadly, the people did not listen to the prophets God sent. They worshipped false gods and turned their backs on God's love for them. But God stuck to His plan to use His people to bless the world.

A Roaring Rescue

Daniel and the Lions' Den
Daniel 1:1-4; 6

God's people disobeyed Him, so He let their enemies take them into captivity.

They destroyed Jerusalem and carried away many of the Jews to their own country, Babylon.

Daniel was one of the Jews
in Babylon. He trusted God and
prayed to Him three times a day.

God blessed Daniel,

and he became a powerful leader
in that country.

Some leaders were jealous of Daniel, so they made a new law. People could only pray to King Darius.

Whoever disobeyed would
be thrown into a lions' den.
Darius agreed.

Daniel still prayed to God and was arrested. Darius was sad; he liked Daniel. He realized he'd been tricked but couldn't change the law.

Daniel was thrown to the lions.

The lions roared and crept up to Daniel. Then an angel arrived! It was God who sent him. The angel shut the lions' mouths. Daniel spent the night there

unharmed.

At daybreak, Darius went to see if Daniel was alive. "God sent an angel to save me," Daniel said. The king was thrilled. Daniel was pulled out of the den.

Then King Darius had Daniel's enemies thrown into the den. The lions gobbled them up!

King Darius told everyone in his kingdom to honor Daniel's powerful, living God.

Why was Daniel thrown to the lions?

Many years later, in another land,
a brave woman named Esther
trusted and honored God. She
was part of God's plan to protect
His people when they lived
outside the promised land.

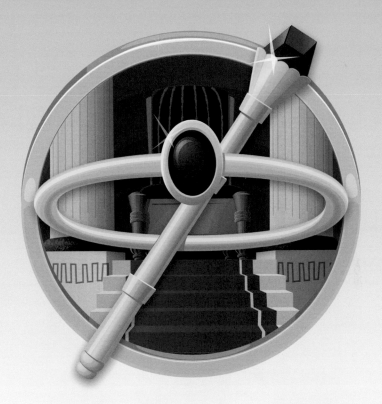

The Brave and Beautiful Queen

Esther
Esther 2-5; 7; 9:20-22

Esther was the Queen of Persia. Even her husband, King Xerxes, didn't know her secret.

Esther was Jewish. Esther's cousin, Mordecai, worked at the palace and looked out for her.

Xerxes' advisor, Haman, received a great reward. He was very proud. Everyone except Mordecai bowed down to him. Haman was insulted.

He vowed to
**kill Mordecai
and all the Jews!**

Haman told Xerxes that the Jews were dangerous and should die. Xerxes agreed and set a day to kill them.

Mordecai was terrified and sent a message to Queen Esther.

"Change the king's mind," said Mordecai. "If I go to him without his invitation, he can have me killed," Esther replied. "Perhaps you were made queen just for this moment," said Mordecai.

Esther bravely agreed to try. She went to the throne room. King Xerxes was amazed by her beauty and invited her in. "Can we have dinner with Haman?" she asked.

Haman was building a big
gallows in his back yard.
He planned to hang
Mordecai on it.

Then the king's invitation arrived.
So Haman went to the palace for dinner.

"A man wants to kill me and my people, the Jews," Esther told Xerxes.

"Who would do such a thing?" he asked.
"The evil Haman!" Esther cried.
"Haman? Guards! Put him to death."

209

So Haman was hanged on the gallows he'd built for Mordecai. Because of Esther, the Jews were saved! They celebrated with a great feast, which they observe to this day.

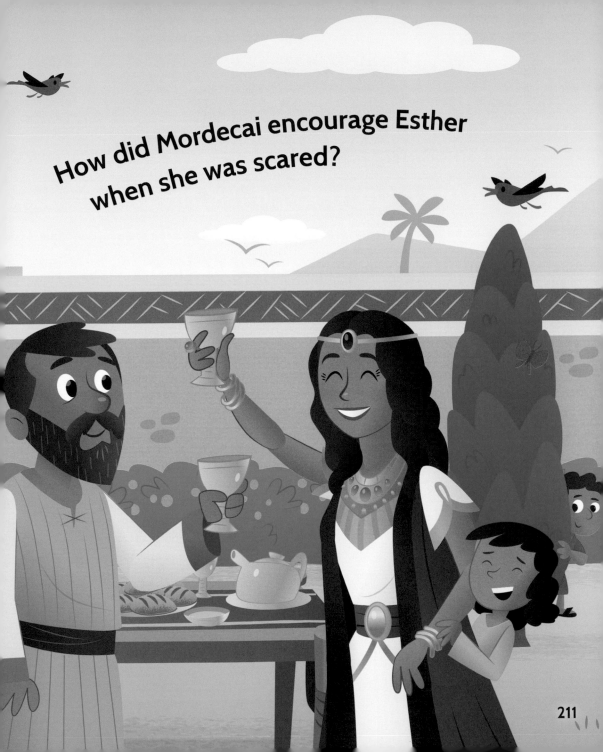

How did Mordecai encourage Esther when she was scared?

211

God kept His promise to His people.
After many years, at just the right
time, the plan God had from the
beginning came true. He sent His
only Son, Jesus, to fix people's
relationship with God
broken by sin.

The First Christmas Gift

Jesus is Born
Luke 1:26-38; 2:1-20; Matthew 1:18-25

The angel, Gabriel, told Mary,
   "You will have a baby!"
"How?" asked Mary. "I'm not married."

"God's Holy Spirit will come down to you. The baby will be God's Son." Mary believed him.

Mary was engaged to Joseph, but he didn't believe her story. So an angel visited him too. "Mary's not lying. Her baby will be God's Son.

You must name
Him Jesus."

Many months passed. Then they traveled
to Bethlehem, Joseph's hometown,
to be counted by the government. After
that long journey,

Mary was ready
to give birth.

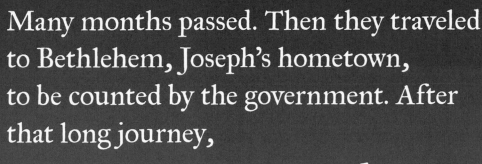

But all the inns in Bethlehem were full.
So God's Son was born in a stable,

wrapped in cloths, and laid on a bed
of hay. They named Him Jesus.

That night, an angel appeared to some shepherds in the hills near Bethlehem. "Good news!" the angel said. "Your Savior has been born. He's in Bethlehem, lying in a manger."

Suddenly more angels appeared, so many
of them that they filled the skies. "Praise God
in heaven!" they all sang. "And may everyone
who pleases Him receive His peace."

When the angels left, the shepherds hurried to Bethlehem. They found the baby, their Savior, lying on a bed of hay. It was just as the first angel had said.

After the shepherds had seen Jesus,
they went through
the town.

They were very excited! They told everyone what had happened, and they praised God for what He had done!

Why were the shepherds so excited?

Jesus grew up. He never sinned, so His relationship with God, His Father, was never broken. Only He could bring people and God back together.

The Beloved Son

Jesus is Baptized
Matthew 3:1-3; 13-17; Luke 3:15-16;
John 1:29; Malachi 3:1

"Before God sends His special Savior," said the prophet Malachi, "a messenger will come to prepare the way for Him."

So John came before Jesus, preaching by the Jordan River.

"Prepare the way for the Lord!"

John said. "God is sending someone very special to His people.

Change your ways. Turn from the bad
things you have done. Be baptized."
So that's what the people did!
"Are you the promised one?" they asked.
"No," said John. "I'm not worthy
to even carry His sandals. He will
do amazing things. You'll see!"

Jesus came to John to be baptized.

When John saw Jesus, he said, "Behold, the Lamb of God who takes away the sins of the world!"

"I want you to baptize Me," Jesus said.
"No," John replied. "I need to be baptized
by You!"

"Trust Me," said Jesus.
"This is the right thing to do."

So John baptized Jesus. God's
Spirit came down on Jesus like
a dove. "This is My Son," God said.
"I love Him.

He pleases Me very much!"

How did God show His love for His Son?

Jesus is God's Son, but He still
understands our weaknesses.
He was tempted to do wrong
things, just like us.

240

A Test in the Desert

Jesus is Tempted
Matthew 4:1-11

God's Spirit led Jesus into the desert. He had nothing to eat for forty days and nights.

After that, Jesus was very hungry!

Knowing that Jesus was hungry, Satan tempted Him. He pointed to a rock and said, "If You are the Son of God, tell these rocks to become bread."

Jesus answered Satan using God's words from the Bible. "It's not just bread that keeps people alive," He said. "Their lives also depend on what God says."

Next, Satan took Jesus to the top of the temple. "If You are the Son of God, jump off!

The Scriptures say that God's angels will rescue You."

247

So Jesus used God's Word
to give His second answer.

"Do not put the Lord your God to the test," He said, quoting again from the Bible.

249

Finally, Satan took Jesus to a mountain and showed Him all the world's kingdoms and wealth.

"This can be Yours," he said,
"if You bow down and worship me."

251

"Go away, Satan!" Jesus commanded.
Then He quoted God's Word one more time.

"For it is written, 'Worship the Lord your God and serve Him only.'"

As soon as Jesus said it, Satan left Him. Then angels came and cared for Him. Jesus had faced temptation and hadn't sinned, **not even once.**

How did Jesus resist temptation?

Jesus wanted people to understand what their lives would be like if they followed God, loved Him, and trusted Him. Jesus called this "The Kingdom of God." It wasn't a kingdom with land and borders. It was a way to live.

The King and the Kingdom

The Sermon on the Mount
Matthew 4:23-7:29; John 18:36-37

Jesus traveled, teaching about the Kingdom of Heaven, and crowds followed Him.

They didn't know yet that Jesus is the King, but He taught them how to live as people of His Kingdom.

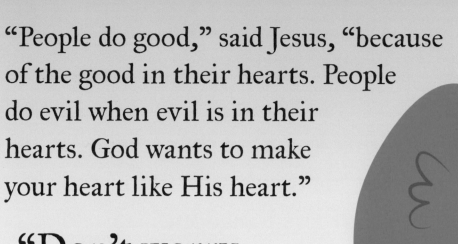

"People do good," said Jesus, "because of the good in their hearts. People do evil when evil is in their hearts. God wants to make your heart like His heart."

"**Don't worry** about things like food and clothes," said Jesus.

"Put God first in your life. Obey Him. Trust Him. He will make sure that you have what you need."

Jesus taught this prayer: "Father God, Your name is holy. Reign on earth like You reign in heaven. Meet our needs today. Help us obey You.

All power is
Yours, forever!"

263

Then Jesus told a story. "One man built his house on a rock. A big storm came. Because the house was built on a rock,

265

"Another man built his house on soft
and shifting sand. A big storm came.

Because the house was built on sand, it fell down with a crash!"

267

"The things I teach you are like the rock," said Jesus.

"Put My words into action,

and you will be like the man
who built his house on a rock."

How can we be like the wise man who built his house on a rock?

Everywhere He went, Jesus not only taught people about God's Kingdom, He also healed people from disease and illness. Jesus cared both for people's hearts and their bodies.

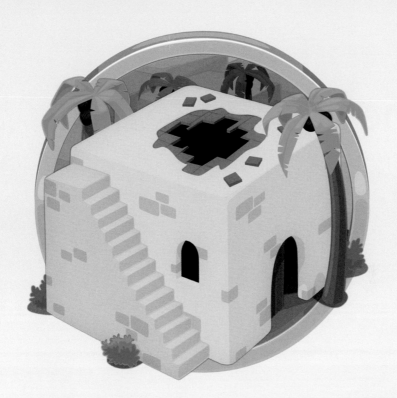

Through the Roof

Jesus Heals a Paralytic Man
Luke 5:17-26

Full!
The house was full!

Jesus was in the house teaching and healing, and everyone wanted to see Him.

Some men had a friend
who could not walk.

They believed that Jesus could heal him, so they carried him to the house on a mat.

Because the house was so full,
**they couldn't
get in.**

So they carried their friend up the steps
to the flat roof and started tearing up the tiles!

They opened a hole in the roof. Everyone in the house looked up,

amazed!

Then they lowered their friend into the middle of the crowd.

They thought Jesus would heal their friend. Instead, Jesus said to him, "Your sins are forgiven." The religious leaders were very unhappy.

"Only God can forgive sins," they grumbled.

"What's easier?" asked Jesus. "To forgive a man's sins or make him walk? To show you that I have God's power to forgive sins, I will heal his legs."

"Pick up your mat and walk home," said Jesus to the man. And he did! His friends cheered and so did everyone else.

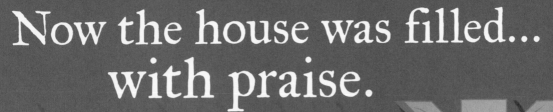

Now the house was filled... with praise.

Why were the religious leaders very unhappy with Jesus?

Jesus healed sick people. He calmed a storm at sea. He walked on water. Through these miracles, and more, He showed the people that He was the Savior God sent. In Jesus they saw God's love and power.

The Big Picnic

Jesus Feeds 5,000
Mark 6:30-44

Jesus had finished teaching. Everyone was hungry. "Send them away to buy food," His disciples said.

But Jesus wanted to show the people that they could trust God.

287

"It would take a year's wages to buy bread for them all!" His disciples cried. "How much food do you have?" asked Jesus.

"There is a boy here," said Andrew, "who has five loaves of bread and two little fish." Jesus smiled. "Perfect. Tell the people to sit down on the grass."

So the people sat down all over the mountainside. Jesus thanked God for the bread and the fish. Then He broke them into pieces for His disciples to hand out.

Jesus' disciples passed out bread and fish to the whole crowd. There were five thousand men and lots of women and children too.

Everyone ate as much as they wanted!

Afterwards, the disciples gathered up the leftovers. There were twelve baskets full from just five loaves and two fish!

The people knew they could trust God to care for them.

How did Jesus show the people that they could trust God?

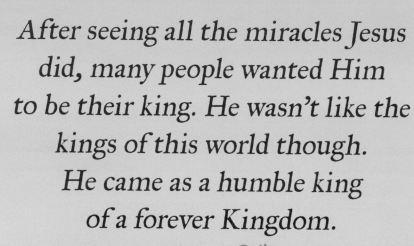

After seeing all the miracles Jesus
did, many people wanted Him
to be their king. He wasn't like the
kings of this world though.
He came as a humble king
of a forever Kingdom.

The Donkey and the King

The Triumphal Entry
Matthew 21:1-11; John 12:16-19; Luke 19:36-40

It was Passover time. Jerusalem was filled with people.

When Jesus reached the Mount of Olives, a hill overlooking Jerusalem, He told two of His disciples to find a donkey.

They found the donkey and put their cloaks on it. Jesus rode on the donkey, fulfilling the Bible verse that says, "Here comes your King, Jerusalem, riding on a donkey."

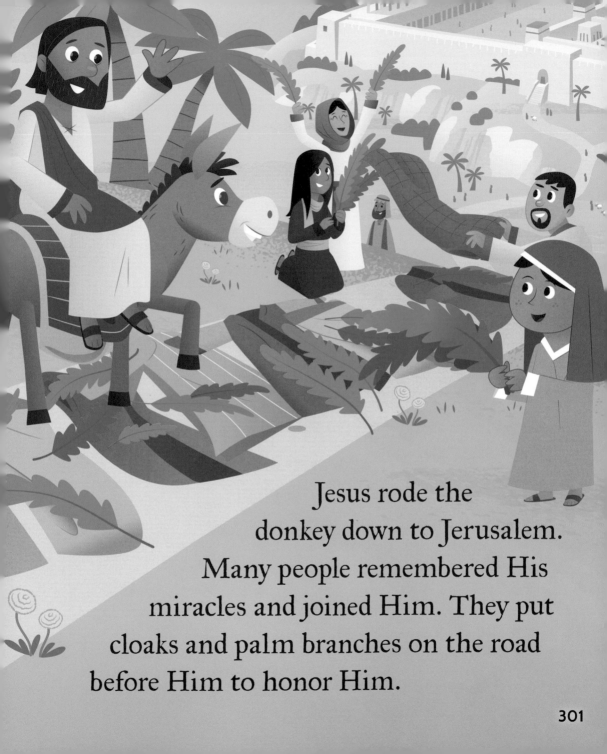

Jesus rode the donkey down to Jerusalem. Many people remembered His miracles and joined Him. They put cloaks and palm branches on the road before Him to honor Him.

They hoped that Jesus was God's promised Savior. So they shouted,

"Hosanna!"

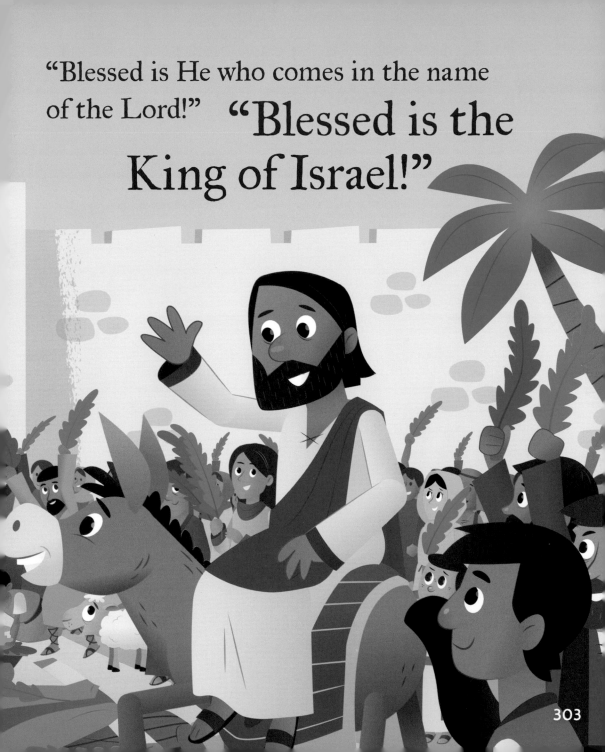

"Blessed is He who comes in the name of the Lord!" "Blessed is the King of Israel!"

"The whole world is following Him," the Pharisees grumbled. "Tell them to be quiet, Jesus!"

"Even if everyone stopped shouting," Jesus replied, "the stones would still praise Me!"

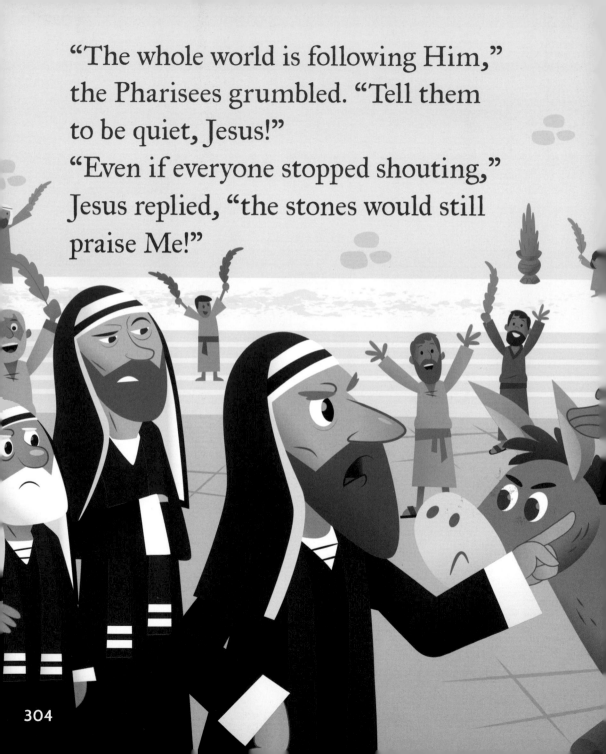

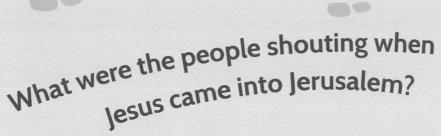

What were the people shouting when Jesus came into Jerusalem?

Jesus knew that it was time for Him
to leave the world and to go back
to His Father. Before He left,
He wanted His disciples to know
He loved them no matter what.

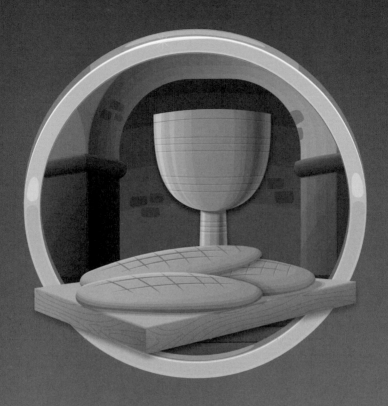

A Goodbye Meal

The Last Supper
Matthew 26:14-16; John 13:26-30;
Mark 14:12-26

Jesus healed sick people and fed hungry people. He loved outcasts and taught everyone about God's Kingdom.

But the religious leaders didn't like
His teaching and were jealous of Him.

They hated Jesus so much that they decided to have Him killed.

They gave thirty pieces of silver
to Judas, one of Jesus' disciples,
to hand Jesus over to them.

Then Jesus and His disciples celebrated the Passover. While they ate, Jesus said sadly, "One of you will betray Me." Surprised, they each replied, "It's not me, Lord!"

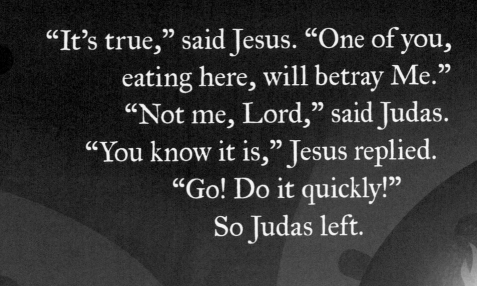

"It's true," said Jesus. "One of you,
eating here, will betray Me."
"Not me, Lord," said Judas.
"You know it is," Jesus replied.
"Go! Do it quickly!"
So Judas left.

Jesus took bread and thanked God for it. He broke it, gave it to His disciples, and said, "Remember Me when you eat this.

It's My body,
given for you."

Then Jesus picked up a cup and thanked God for it. "Everyone drink from this cup,"

He said, "This is My blood, poured out so that sins may be forgiven."

When they had finished eating, Jesus and His disciples sang a hymn together. Then they walked to the Garden of Gethsemane to pray.

What did Jesus say about the bread and the cup?

Jesus prayed in the garden, "My Father! Your will be done, not mine." Then, the religious leaders came with soldiers to arrest Him and take Him to trial. And all His disciples ran away.

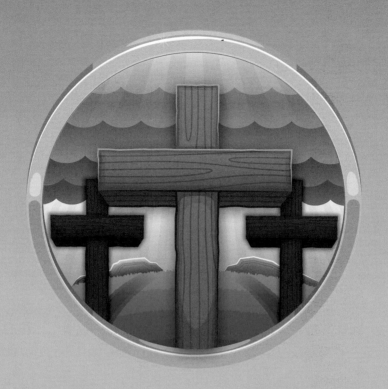

It is Finished

The Cross
John 18:28–19:42; Luke 23:34–35

The religious leaders told the governor, Pilate, that Jesus was dangerous and wanted to be king.

Pilate asked Jesus, "Is this true?"

"I am king," Jesus answered,
"but not of this world."

323

"Jesus is innocent," said Pilate. "There's no reason to kill Him.

I will set Him free." But the crowd shouted, **"Kill Him!"**

So Pilate had his soldiers whip Jesus.
They forced a thorny crown on His head.

Then they laid a wooden cross on His back and led Him up a hill.

There on that hill, the Roman soldiers nailed Jesus to the cross — hands and feet. Then they raised it high. Jesus hung there between two criminals. Around noon, the sky turned dark. Jesus' friends wept. The religious leaders

laughed and said, "You saved other people. Why can't You save Yourself?"

"**Forgive them, Father,**" said Jesus.

When the time came for Jesus
to die, He closed His eyes and said,

"It is finished."

He had completed what He had
come to do because of His great love.

One of Jesus' followers, a man named Joseph, put Jesus' body in a brand new tomb. He rolled a huge stone in front of it.

A long, sad Friday was over.

Why did Jesus die on the cross?

333

Jesus' death on the cross was not a defeat. It was God's plan. When Jesus died, He took the punishment for our sins to fix our broken relationship with God. Jesus promised something special would happen on the third day after He died.

A Happy Sunday!

The Empty Tomb
Mark 16:1-4; Matthew 28:5-8;
John 20:3-10; Luke 24:1-12; 36-49

Sunday morning, some women went to put burial spices on Jesus' body.

They knew a big stone was covering the tomb's entrance and wondered how they would move it.

When they arrived, the stone had already been moved, Jesus' body was gone, and there were angels in the tomb!

"Jesus is alive!"
the angels said. "Go tell His disciples."

The women told the disciples, and
Peter and John ran to Jesus' tomb
to see for themselves.

All they found were Jesus' burial
cloths. They went back home, confused.

Later, the disciples were gathered together in a room. They were talking about what had happened when Jesus appeared to them. They were terrified. They thought He was a ghost.

"Don't worry,"

said Jesus. "See my hands and feet. It's me! Touch me! Go on! You can't touch a ghost. And ghosts don't eat either, but I'm feeling really hungry."

343

So He ate some fish. Then He taught them. "The Scriptures are clear," He said.

"The Messiah was supposed to suffer and die, and **then be raised from the dead.**"

345

"Now tell the world what you have seen. Let everyone know that their sins can be forgiven if they turn to God! It's possible because of what I have done."

What did the women find when they went to the tomb?

Jesus appeared to 500 of His followers over the next forty days, and proved that He was actually alive. He also talked to them about the Kingdom of God.

Into the Clouds

Jesus Returns to Heaven
Matthew 28:18-20; Acts 1:4-12

It was time for Jesus to go to heaven. He led His disciples to the top of a mountain near Jerusalem.

"Here's what I want you to do," He said.

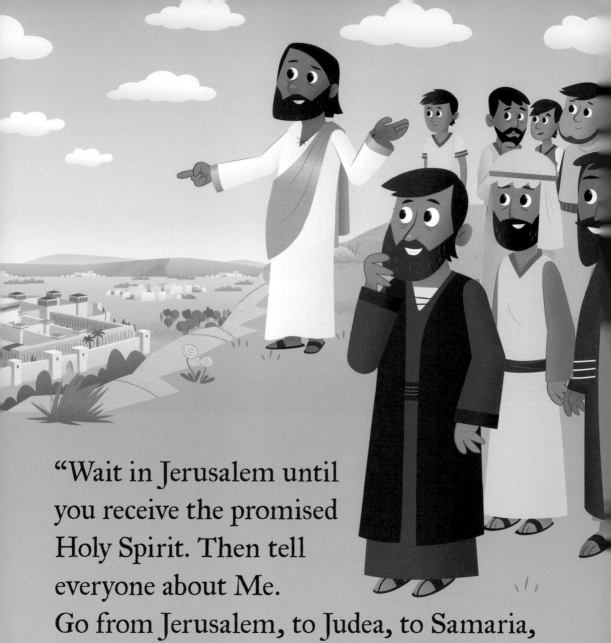

"Wait in Jerusalem until you receive the promised Holy Spirit. Then tell everyone about Me. Go from Jerusalem, to Judea, to Samaria, and then to the rest of the world!"

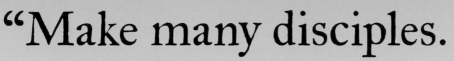

"Make many disciples. Baptize them in the name of the Father, the Son, and the Holy Spirit. Teach them everything you learned from Me. I will always be with you."

When He had said this, Jesus rose into the sky. Up He went until **He disappeared into a cloud.**

His disciples watched Him. They stood there staring into the sky.

Two men, dressed in white, appeared.
"Jesus has gone to heaven," they explained.
"He will come back in the same way!"
So the disciples obeyed Jesus and went
to Jerusalem.

What did Jesus tell His disciples
to do before He went to heaven?

Before He left, Jesus promised His disciples He would send someone to help them. That someone was God's Holy Spirit. He would help them understand the truth about Jesus.

God's Wonderful Gift

The Holy Spirit Comes
Acts 2:1-47

Jews from all over the world were in Jerusalem for the Feast of Pentecost. Jesus' followers were there too.

They gathered together, waiting for the gift Jesus had promised them.

In the middle of the festival,
God's gift arrived.

It began with a sound, a sound like a howling wind that filled the house where they were waiting.

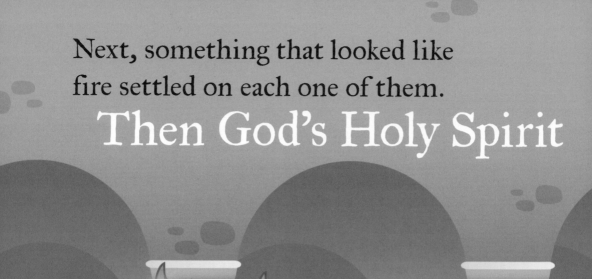

Next, something that looked like
fire settled on each one of them.
Then God's Holy Spirit

filled everyone in the room,

and He gave them power to speak different languages!

Jews from other parts of the world heard them and were amazed. "These people are speaking our languages," they said,

"and proclaiming the wonderful things God has done!"

"This is God's gift," Peter explained. "It was promised long ago. It comes to us through Jesus, the Messiah. You crucified Him, but God brought Him back to life."

"What should we do?" the people asked sadly.
"Turn away from evil," said Peter.
"Believe in Jesus Christ.
He will forgive your sins and give you
His Holy Spirit."

On that day, three thousand people were baptized. They were just the first of many people who would come to trust in Jesus as their Savior.

What did Peter say would happen if we believe in Jesus?

When those 3,000 people were baptized, they became members of God's family, the Church. With the Holy Spirit's power, the disciples taught about Jesus and even performed miracles. Many more people believed in Jesus.

From Enemy to Friend

Paul meets Jesus
Acts 9:1–19

S aul was a religious man, a Pharisee. He thought that anyone who believed in Jesus

was spreading a lie and should be
put in prison and even put to death.

Saul was going to Damascus to arrest Jesus' followers. Suddenly, a bright light surrounded him. He fell down. A voice said, "Saul, why are you so cruel to Me?"

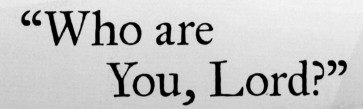

"Who are You, Lord?"

Saul asked. The voice replied, "I am Jesus, the one you want to harm. Go to Damascus. There you will learn what you must do."

Saul got up, but he was blind.

His friends led him to a house in Damascus. Saul waited there for three days. He had nothing to eat or drink.

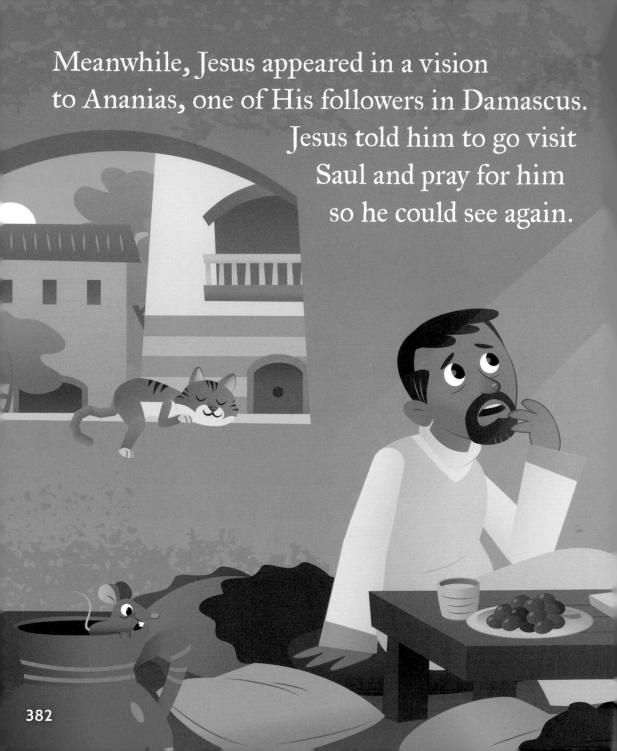

Meanwhile, Jesus appeared in a vision to Ananias, one of His followers in Damascus. Jesus told him to go visit Saul and pray for him so he could see again.

But Saul wants to arrest Your followers," Ananias said trembling. "I know," said Jesus, "but I want to use Saul to tell people all over the world about Me."

Ananias went to pray for Saul. "Jesus sent me," he said, "so that you may see and be filled with the Holy Spirit."

Saul could see again!

Then he was baptized.

Jesus changed Saul from a man who hurt His followers to a church leader who told everyone about Jesus! So He changed his name, as well, to Paul.

What changed
in Saul's life after he met Jesus?

By the same power that brought
Jesus back from the dead, God will
one day make all things new.
Jesus will return just like God's Word
promises, and those who believe
in Jesus will live with Him forever.

A Forever Promise

The New Heaven and the New Earth
Revelation 1:17-18; 21:1-7

John was a disciple of Jesus. One day, Jesus came to him in a vision, shining like the sun. "Don't be afraid," said Jesus. "I died. Now I live forever!"

Then John saw a new
heaven and a new earth,

God's promised
new creation.

The first heaven and the first earth
were gone and the sea with them!

Next, John saw

God's Holy City,
the new Jerusalem.

It was coming down from heaven. It was beautiful, like a bride on her wedding day ready to meet her husband!

Then John heard a loud voice coming from the throne of God saying, "From now on, God will make His home among

His people, and they will
all live together."

"In this new heaven and new earth, there won't be any tears because no one will be in pain, and no one will die."

"Those things are gone forever!"

Then the voice from the throne said, "I am **the Beginning and the End.**

If you are thirsty, come to me, and **I will give you the water of life.**"

"My new world is for my children, those who are faithful to me. I'm making all things new.

It's true.

You can count on it."

What are you looking forward to in the new world God promises?

God's Good News

Be Part of the Story

In the beginning, God made everything! He made it perfect. He made us too, in His image. He loves us and wants to have a relationship with us.

Sadly, Adam and Eve disobeyed God.
That sin brought death into the world
and broke our relationship with God.
It also broke God's perfect world.

Sin spread throughout the whole world.
Everyone sins, and the result of sin is death.
But sin couldn't stop God from loving us.

He had a plan!

Because of His love for us, God sent His Son, Jesus, into the world. Sin broke our relationship with God, but Jesus came to fix it!

Jesus healed sick people and performed many other miracles! He welcomed lonely people. He taught people about God's love. His perfect life shows us what love looks like.

Even though Jesus never sinned. He died on a cross for our sins because He loves us. By doing this, He was carrying out God's plan to fix our relationship with Him.

Three days later, Jesus rose from the dead, breaking the power of sin and death! He spent time with His followers, teaching them. Then He returned to Heaven.

Now Jesus lives forever!

Jesus did not leave us alone.

He sent His Holy Spirit to live inside everyone who trusts Him. The Spirit gives us power to live the way God created us to live.

One day, when Jesus returns, God will make everything perfect again. He will make a New Heaven and a New Earth. Everyone who trusts in Jesus will live with Him forever!

God loves you. He created you one-of-a-kind!
Trusting and following Jesus fixes our broken
relationship with God!

Are you ready to be
a part of God's story?

Continue the Journey...

You've reached the end of this book, but God's Story is not over! There is so much more to learn! All the stories you've just read are part of an app called the *Bible App for Kids*. Get the FREE interactive app!

What is the *Bible App for Kids?*

Created by YouVersion and OneHope, the *Bible App for Kids* is sharing God's Story with children around the world.

You can view the stories in this book, as well as many more. All Bible stories are animated with music, narration, and fun activities!

It is the most-downloaded children's Bible app of all time.

Available in several languages, the app is regularly updated to reach even more kids around the world in their heart language.

BibleAppforKids.com

FREE resources for parents are available so your whole family can engage with the app, as well as a Sunday School curriculum so your church can get involved! Resources include:

- Video Episodes
- Family Devotionals
- Coloring Pages
- Activity Sheets

- *Bible App for Kids* Curriculum
  - Ages 2 to Pre-K
  - Original, downloadable songs
  - Live-Action hosts
  - Animated characters
  - Memory verses with motions
  - Leader training video

Download the FREE interactive app
The Bible App for Kids • bible.com/kids

YouVersion helps you engage with the Bible through free apps like the *Bible App* and the *Bible App for Kids*. Whether you're a frequent or first-time reader of the Bible, the apps give you a meaningful experience in God's Word without the interruption of ads. YouVersion is a ministry of LifeChurch.tv, a multi-site church based in Oklahoma. Meeting in locations throughout the U.S. and globally online at live.LifeChurch.tv, our church is devoted to leading people across the planet to become fully devoted followers of Christ. Get the world's most popular *Bible App* at bible.com/app and visit bible.com/kids to download the free *Bible App for Kids*.

OneHope®
GOD'S WORD. EVERY CHILD.

OneHope is an international ministry that reaches children and youth around the world with God's Word – more than a billion kids in 145 countries have encountered a OneHope Scripture program since 1987! To create age-specific and culturally-relevant Scripture programs, OneHope conducts research with children and youth, leaders and educators in the different countries it works. By collaborating with thousands of local churches and ministries, local governments, schools and non-governmental organizations, OneHope plans to reach every child with God's Word. onehope.net